The Yes Plan
Empowered through Budgeting!

By DeLisa Lovett

The Yes Plan
Empowered through Budgeting!

By DeLisa Lovett

Copyright © 2024 by DeLisa Lovett

All rights reserved.

"The Yes Plan – Empowered through Budgeting" is a work of non-fiction. Names, characters, places, and incidents are products of the author's experiences. Any resemblance to actual events, locales, organizations, or persons, living or dead, is entirely accurate.

No part of this book may be reproduced, distributed, or transmitted in any form or by any means, including photocopying, recording, or other electronic or mechanical methods, without the express written permission of the author and publisher, except for the use of brief quotations in a book review as permitted by copyright law.

ISBN: 9798309714766

DEDICATION

I dedicate this book to all the brilliant and intelligent people that have authored books that I have read and yet to read. I appreciate "words" and hope this book will inspire others to author their own book or just enjoy reading this one and many more. Thanks to God!

DISCLOSURE

This information is for reference material only, therefore claims based on plagiarism or misinformation by author DeLisa Lovett or business Lovett Investments, LLC is not subject to liability for incidental consequential, punitive, or other similar damages associated with this information.

This information is compiled from multiple public sources available at the time of this writing.

Be sure to consult an Attorney, CPA, or licensed Financial Advisors on any legal and/or financial matters regarding the business.

CONTENTS

	Acknowledgments	I
1	The 3 W's	7
2	Introduction of "The Yes Plan"	9
3	Importance of Budgeting	11
4	Setting SMART goals	14
5	"The Yes Plan" Mindset	17
6	"The Yes Plan" Budget	20
7	Savings and Investments	24
8	Budget Applications and Rules	27
9	Making Adjustments	35
10	Increase Income Opportunities	39
11	Celebrating Financial Wins	42
12	Yes to Your Financial Future	44

ACKNOWLEDGMENTS

I give thanks to God, all my friends and family. I want to give a special thanks to my family and friends for the motivation to continue to write and publish this book. Thanks for the inspiration, dedication, perseverance, and support.

DeLisa Lovett

The 3 W's

1 The 3 W's

Who Am I?
Hello, my name is DeLisa, pronounced as D Lisa.

What makes you qualified or credible to share financial information?

I received my bachelor's degree in business administration in 2010. I worked in various departments at a major bank for 10+ years afterward. I started as a Customer Service Representative at a local branch and eventually moved upward to the Home Equity department as Assistant Supervisor as Loan Quality Reviewer.

I am a business owner since 2015. Although inactive, I also received my Wisconsin life insurance license and a Wisconsin Notary Stamp.

I have also actively participated in a real estate group and have read several financial books by successful financial mentors.

What is your Goal?
I aim to share my knowledge about financial matters based on my own individual experiences to help other people and/or businesses while making a profitable living.

Why share?
To fulfill my purpose of teaching other people and new businesses in financial matters to take action **today** to succeed.

DeLisa Lovett

Introduction of "The Yes Plan"

2 Introduction of "The Yes Plan"

Money and budgeting are essential parts of life that can assist you in succeeding financially in your personal and/or business life.

The budget can help you visualize and understand exactly where your money is coming in (income) and going out (expenses).

In this book on budgeting, you will learn about a new approach called "The Yes Plan."

This method focuses on shifting your mindset towards a positive and proactive approach to managing your finances.

Instead of cringing at the word **"budget,"** thinking negatively, and being restricted by it, "The Yes Plan" encourages you to say "Yes" to your financial goals, thinking positively and realistically, and making smart financial decisions with your money.

By adopting "The Yes Plan" mindset, you will gain confidence in your ability to control and manage your finances and make empowered decisions about your future.

DeLisa Lovett

Importance of Budgeting

3 Importance of Budgeting

Every successful person and/or business usually has a plan that includes a mission statement or goals to achieve, key personnel and metrics, and a financial forecast of its future.

A business plan is a blueprint for successful businesses, and a budget is a blueprint for successful individuals.

"The Yes Plan" will help you by creating a budget that shows how you will receive, spend, save, and invest your money.

You can identify your income, track your expenses, and identify areas where you should allocate funds based on your priorities and goals, such as housing, transportation, daycare, emergencies, retirement, education, savings, and investing.

Budgeting prepares you for unexpected expenses, allows you to take advantage of financial opportunities, and allows you to make informed decisions about your money.

"The Yes Plan" creates a budget that aligns with your values, priorities, mission, and goals. Learn how to set realistic financial goals, track spending, and adjust as needed to stay on track.

Without a budget, it is easy to overspend and accumulate debt, causing stress and worry.

With "The Yes Plan", anyone can take control of their finances, reduce financial stress, and build a strong financial foundation for the future.

It helps you to live within your means, maximize savings, and be empowered with money by making intelligent and informed financial decisions for your future.

Setting SMART Goals

4 Setting SMART Goals

Understanding your values, priorities, and goals about your budget is key to successfully managing your finances.

By the end of this chapter, you will clearly understand the importance of setting SMART goals.

SMART is a memory tool designed to establish criteria for setting goals, developed by George T. Doran in 1981.

By setting (SMART) specific, measurable, achievable, relevant, and time-bound goals, you can create an empowering budget for your financial success.

Specific means the goal should be clear and defined. For example, vacation to Italy instead of vacation.

Measurable means the goal should have success points. For example, for a $10,000 saving goal, determine when $5,000 is saved at the midway point and then at the success point when $10,000 is saved.

Achievable means the goal can be obtained and completed. For example, saving $10,000 for a vacation to Italy.

Relevant means the goal should be based on your values and priorities. For example, a vacation to Italy may be included in your love of traveling.

Time-bound means the goal should be achieved within a defined time of completion. For example, a vacation to Italy in 2 years.

In the example above, the SMART goal is saving $10,000 for a vacation to Italy in 2 years because you love traveling. At the midpoint assessment at 1 year, $5000 was saved.

Setting SMART goals will help you develop a personalized plan that aligns with your values and priorities and helps you stay on track with your financial plans.

DeLisa Lovett

"The Yes Plan" Mindset

5 "The Yes Plan" Mindset

Setting SMART goals will help you stay motivated and focused on your financial journey and empower you to make informed decisions about managing your money.

When setting SMART goals for "The Yes Plan", it's essential to consider both short-term (minor purchases) and long-term (major purchases) goals.

Short-term goals include saving for an expensive dinner or emergency fund. A short-term goal is defined as one that is achieved within 3-6 months.

For example, an expensive dinner may cost less than $100 and can fit comfortably within the budget as a short-term goal.

The "Yes" comes easy because the amount is small and obtainable, and the short-term goal can be achieved quickly.

Long-term goals include saving for vacation, retirement, or buying a house. A long-term goal is defined as one that is achieved within 6-24 months or longer.

For example, a vacation that costs $5000 or more may not comfortably fit within the budget.

At this point, the mind may say, "No," "Not Yet," "I don't know," "We will see," "It costs too much," or use any other excuse.

These excuses are why people cringe at the thought of the word "budget," view it negatively and restrictively, and, therefore, don't budget.

But this is the best opportunity to say "Yes" to your priorities and goals.

These goals must be long-term goals and placed in the budget as future purchases.

To achieve the $5000 long-term goal, you could break the goal down into $200 increments for 25 months within the budget.

"The Yes Plan" is a new mindset that views the word "budget" as good, positive, and unrestrictive, and it leads to budgeting.

Say "Yes" to your future major purchases and long-term goals, empowering your mind and financial life with "The Yes Plan's" new mindset.

"The Yes Plan" lets you know when your short-term or long-term goal will be achieved, whether it's an expensive dinner, emergency fund, shopping trip, vacation, or buying a house because you have taken control of your financial decisions.

The "Yes" also gives you the satisfaction of success that your SMART goal was achieved.

"The Yes Plan" mindset will help you make smart financial decisions for future short-term (minor purchases) and long-term (major purchases) goals.

"The Yes Plan" mindset allows you to take control of your financial future and achieve the life you desire.

"The Yes Plan" Budget

6 "The Yes Plan" Budget

Developing "The Yes Plan" budget is essential to financial planning to help you control and manage your finances, set priorities, and achieve your financial goals.

This chapter will discuss the importance of identifying and understanding your income (incoming money), expenses (outgoing money), and savings (money kept) when creating a practical budget.

By identifying these key factors, it's extremely important to be honest with yourself about your finances. Honesty will help you make smarter financial decisions about the priorities and goals you want to achieve.

The key is to write **everything** down accordingly.

"The Yes Plan" can help you make smart financial decisions about your priorities, needs, wants, and goals you want to achieve.

Income is money coming in, for personal households or businesses, including employment salary, wages, bonuses, social security, investments, child support, business revenue, invoices, etc.

Expenses are money going out from personal households or businesses.

Understanding the difference between two types of expenses, fixed and variable expenses, is also important.

Fixed expenses are costs that remain the same each month, cover your basic needs, **and** are non-negotiable.

Fixed expenses include rent or mortgage, car payments, utilities, transportation, health insurance, and life insurance.

Variable expenses, on the other hand, are costs that can fluctuate from month to month, cover your wants, and are flexible.

Variable expenses such as groceries, dining out, and entertainment.

Charity giving can be either fixed or variable based on personal preferences and religious beliefs.

Savings are holding money for personal household or business for future purposes.

Savings help build a financial cushion for emergencies, retirement, children/grandchildren or godchildren for education, future business, savings, and future major purchases.

Unexpected events such as medical emergencies, car repairs, or job loss can significantly impact your finances if you are unprepared.

When planning for financial emergencies, it is vital to have an emergency savings fund to cover unexpected expenses.

Save at least 3-6 months' worth of living expenses in a savings account.

Regularly review and update your emergency plan to ensure it aligns with your current financial situation and goals.

Accurately identifying your income, expenses, and savings can create a realistic Yes budget that aligns with your priorities and goals.

Key phrases that you will begin to use confidently, positively, and assertively are "I have a budget," "Let me check my budget," and most importantly, "My budget empowers me to live my best life."

"The Yes Plan" helps you determine your future needs and wants, allowing you to look forward to planned activities with certainty, positivity, and smart financial decision-making.

Therefore, the word "<u>budget</u>" becomes a good word: positive, unrestrictive, and practical, "The Yes Plan."

Understanding your financial situation is the first step towards financial stability and success.

Savings and Investments

7 Savings and Investments

Another essential aspect of budgeting is allocating funds for savings and investments.

Savings help build a financial cushion for unexpected emergencies, while investments help grow your wealth over time.

One of the key components of savings is planning for financial emergencies.

Having an emergency savings account is important to cover unexpected expenses by saving at least 3-6 months' worth of living expenses.

Unexpected events such as medical emergencies, car repairs, or job loss can significantly impact your finances if you are unprepared financially to pay for them.

By creating a solid plan for these emergencies, you can help alleviate the stress and financial strain they may bring.

Regularly review and update your emergency plan to ensure it aligns with your current financial situation and goals.

By adequately placing funds in an emergency savings account, you can secure your financial future and work towards achieving your financial goals.

Understanding what you are saving and investing for will help you determine your priorities and set SMART goals.

Investments help grow your wealth over time.

Consider diversifying your investment portfolio to reduce risk and maximize returns over the long term.

Your investment portfolio can include funds in a 401k, Roth IRA, money market savings accounts, stocks and bonds, real estate, art, and gold, among other things.

By adequately placing funds in these areas, you can secure your financial future and work towards achieving your financial goals.

Review the budget to ensure funds are going toward savings and investments.

Additionally, consider obtaining adequate rental and/or property insurance coverage to protect yourself against financial losses.

DeLisa Lovett

Budget Applications and Rules

8 Budget Applications and Rules

As technology continues to evolve, managing our finances is becoming easier than ever, thanks to budgeting applications and tools for tracking income, expenses, and savings.

These tools can assist individuals in tracking their expenses, creating budgets, setting financial goals, and even monitoring their credit scores.

By incorporating these applications into your daily routine, you can better understand your financial habits and make smarter decisions with your money.

Various budgeting applications and tools are available on the market, each offering unique features to help users manage their money effectively.

Options may include templates in Word, Mint, Empower, purchased in a store or online, or handwritten and generated in a notebook.

These applications can synchronize with your bank accounts, categorize expenses, provide spending insights, and even send alerts when you exceed your budget.

Some tools offer personalized recommendations to help you save more and pay off debt faster.

DeLisa Lovett

MONTHLY BUDGET

JAN	FEB	MAR	APR	MAY	JUN	JUL	AUG	SEP	OCT	NOV	DEC

INCOME 1	INCOME 1	OTHER INCOME	TOTAL INCOME

FIXED EXPENSES	BUDGETED	ACTUAL	VARIABLE EXPENSES	BUDGETED	ACTUAL

DEBT/SAVINGS	BUDGETED	ACTUAL		BUDGETED	ACTUAL
			TOTAL INCOME		
			FIXED EXPENSES		
			VARIABLE EXPENSES		
			DEBT/SAVINGS		
			TOTAL LEFTOVER		

The Budget Rules 50/30/20% or 70/20/10% are guidelines for successfully managing the "Yes" plan for smart financial decision-making.

The budget rules help you categorize funds based on your personal or business needs, wants, savings, and giving goals.

The budget rules are adjustable according to your needs, wants, and savings goals, such as 60/30/10%.

Example: 70/20/10% (Needs/Wants/Savings)

70% Needs

- 30% Housing
- 10% Transportation, Gas, Insurance
- 20% Groceries, Utilities, Life Insurance, Health Insurance, Day Care
- 10% Charity Giving

20% Wants

- 10% Major Purchases
- 10% Vacations and other Luxuries

10% Savings

- 5% Emergency Money (6-12 months)
- 5% Retirement Money, Children's Education/Future Business/Savings

Needs are fixed expenses that cover your basic needs, which include housing, groceries, utilities, transportation, and clothing.

Housing should be approximately 30% or less of your income.

Transportation, gas, and auto insurance should be 10% or less of your income.

Groceries, utilities (light/gas), life insurance, health insurance, daycare, etc., should be less than 20% of your income.

Charity giving can be either fixed as a need or variable as a want, based on personal preferences and religious beliefs.

Charity giving usually is approximately 10% of your income.

Wants are variable expenses that cover wants and luxuries such as entertainment, travel, vacations, and other luxuries.

Major purchases should be 10% or less of your income, while vacations and other luxury expenses should be less than 10% of your income.

Savings can be both fixed and variable expenses that cover future purposes for emergencies, retirement, children/grandchildren or godchildren for education, future business, and savings, as well as future major purchases.

Emergency savings should be 5% or more of your income until the goal of 3-6 months saved is reached.

Your retirement money, children/grandchildren's and godchildren's future college education, future business, and savings should be approximately 5% of your income.

These percentages within the budget rules are adjustable for each personal household or business to be determined accordingly.

For example, a personal household without daycare needs because the children are now grown up or have no children or grandchildren can use 10% toward future emergency savings or retirement savings, increase charity giving from 10% to 20%, or even increase housing from 30% to 40%.

Based on the budget created, it's possible that, additional income may also be needed to cover some expenses and savings goals and say " yes" to major purchases, vacations, and other luxury items.

Now, let's determine which budget rule will be most effective for your "The Yes Plan" budget.

Calculate the housing ratio. Housing payment divided by income equals a decimal number, which is then multiplied by 100 to equal a percentage.

Example: $600/4000 = 0.15 \times 100 = 15\%$ or $2000/10000 = 0.20 \times 100 = 20\%$ or $2000/4000 = 0.50 \times 100 = 50\%$.

If the housing ratio exceeds 50% of the budget, then some decisions may need to be made.

Housing costs exceeding 50% of the income may be unsustainable in the long term; however, there are solutions to this problem.

For example, if you live in an expensive major market city, you may need to get a roommate, move outside city limits, move to another town or state, or increase your income to lower the housing cost.

If you decide not to reduce the housing ratio, then your housing costs should not exceed 50% of the income because other needs must be met.

Ideally, housing costs should be at or lower than 30% of the income.

Calculate the transportation ratio. Next, calculate the transportation ratio to include gas and insurance per month.

Auto payment plus gas plus auto insurance divided by income equals a decimal number, which is then multiplied by 100 to equal a percentage.

Example: $200+100+100/4000 = 0.10 \times 100 = 10\%$ or $400+200+200/4000 = 0.20 \times 100 = 20\%$.

If transportation costs exceed 10% of the income, some decisions may need to be made again.

Transportation costs should not exceed 20% of the income because other needs must be met.

A better budget solution may be to use the budget rule 70/20/10% or another version based on your priorities and goals.

Calculate the other ratios accordingly.

Payment divided by income equals a decimal number, then multiplied by 100 equals the percentage.

Example: $400/4000 = 0.10 \times 100 = 10\%$ or $800/4000 = 0.20 \times 100 = 20\%$.

If other items exceed 10% of income, again, some decisions may need to be made.

Other items should not exceed 20% of the budget's income because savings needs must be met.

The Yes Plan

A better budget solution may be to adjust the budget, obtain additional income, reduce some expenses, and adjust savings goals.

Adjustments may be needed to say "Yes" to your financial goals, major purchases, vacations, and other luxury items.

DeLisa Lovett

Making Adjustments

9 Making Adjustments

One key aspect of effective budgeting is finding ways to adjust the budget - "The Yes Plan" for savings or other financial goals.

This chapter will explore four strategies for adjustments to your budget and saying Yes to your financial goals.

One important strategy is regularly monitoring and adjusting your budget by tracking your spending habits.

Monitoring your budget and tracking your expenses consistently for a few months is equally crucial to gaining insight into where your money is spent on things like dining out, shopping, and other variable expenses so you can stay on track with your financial goals.

By keeping a detailed record of where your money is spent each month, you can easily see patterns and identify areas where you may be overspending, allowing you to adjust accordingly.

It also allows you to take control of your finances, make smarter decisions with your money, avoid unnecessary debt, and ultimately reach your financial goals.

Adjusting your budget is essential when unexpected expenses arise or your financial goals change.

By being flexible and proactive in making changes to your budget, you can better adapt to various financial circumstances and avoid financial stress.

Another key strategy is managing debt effectively to achieve financial stability and reach your budgeting goals.

Debt can quickly accumulate if not handled properly, leading to stress and financial difficulties.

One key aspect of managing debt effectively is prioritizing a debt repayment plan in your "The Yes Plan" budget.

By implementing strategic debt management techniques, you can take control of your finances and work towards a debt-free future.

By allocating a portion of your income towards paying off debts each month, you can make steady progress toward becoming debt-free.

Developing good financial habits, such as avoiding unnecessary debt and learning to live within your means, can help prevent future financial struggles.

You can proactively manage debt and work towards a more secure financial future by staying mindful of your spending and savings habits.

Additionally, another strategy is to stick to your "The Yes Plan" budget that you created based on your priorities and goals.

Setting limits for different spending categories can help you stay on track and avoid unnecessary purchases. Refer to Chapter 5 on "The Yes Plan" Mindset.

Lastly, consider exploring other options such as debt consolidation, renegotiating bills, and subscriptions.

Many creditors are willing to work with customers for debt consolidation plans, reduce interest rates, and lower monthly payments.

So, feel free to ask for discounts or explore alternative options.

Remember, knowledge is power when it comes to managing your finances!

DeLisa Lovett

Increase Income Opportunities

10 Increase Income Opportunities

One of the key components of successful budgeting is finding ways to increase your income.

By identifying and taking advantage of opportunities to earn more money, you can achieve your financial goals faster and more effectively.

In this chapter, we will explore various strategies and techniques for boosting income and creating a more secure financial future.

One effective way to increase your income is to seek out additional sources of revenue, such as part-time jobs, freelance work, or side hustles.

These opportunities can provide you with extra cash flow, which you can use to pay off debt, build savings, or invest in your future.

By multiplying your income streams, you can create a more stable financial foundation and decrease your reliance on only one source of income.

Another critical strategy for increasing income is continuously improving your skills and knowledge.

Investing in education or training programs that enhance your qualifications can position you for higher-paying job opportunities and career advancement.

Additionally, networking and building relationships within your industry can lead to new opportunities for growth and income generation.

Celebrating Financial Wins

11 Celebrating Financial Wins

This chapter will discuss the importance of celebrating financial wins along your budgeting journey.

Too often, people focus on the negatives regarding money - debt, bills, and expenses.

However, it's equally important to acknowledge and celebrate the small victories that come with effective budgeting.

By recognizing and celebrating your financial wins, you boost your morale and motivation and create positive reinforcement for sticking to your "The Yes Plan" budget.

Whether paying off a credit card, reaching a savings goal, or simply staying within your budget for the month, take the time to acknowledge and celebrate these achievements, big or small.

Remember, budgeting is a journey, and it's important to acknowledge the progress you've made along the way.

By celebrating your financial wins, you're recognizing your hard work and dedication and setting yourself up for continued success in the future.

Some suggestions for celebrating may include taking a 1–2-day vacation, a spa day, a gourmet dinner, or participating in a hobby activity.

Yes to Your Financial Future

12 Yes to Your Financial Future

"The Yes Plan"—Budgeting: It's important to get started right away and recap the key concepts we've covered throughout this book.

I recommend one personal checking account, two savings accounts, a 401k or IRA retirement savings account, and optionally one savings account for each child/grandchild or godchild for starters to manage the budget successfully.

If you also run a business, I recommend one business checking account and two business savings accounts.

You may consult a licensed CPA, attorney, or financial advisor to obtain their recommendation.

One personal checking account for all income to be directly deposited and expenses to flow out.

Automatic transfers from checking to savings accounts may make savings easier to manage; however, I recommend manually making the transfers or deposits to the savings accounts for the first three months of budgeting.

Doing this manually allows you to visualize and track where the money is spent.

If you have a business, use one business checking account to keep track of income and expenses for the business.

Use two savings accounts: one for emergency savings and one for "Yes" items for future major purchases, vacations, and luxuries.

There are also optional savings accounts for each child, grandchild, or godchild for their future educational, business, and savings purposes.

Use two savings accounts for the business: one for emergency savings and one for future major purchases such as new office equipment, building remodeling, etc.

Most employers offer 401k retirement savings accounts for their employees.

The employer usually directly withdraws money from your paycheck for an account.

Save at least the 3-5% minimum for starters, as the employer usually matches that amount.

Later, you can increase your investments up to 20% or the maximum amount.

Use your "Yes" plan to help you make that decision.

You have learned to say "Yes" to your financial future goals so you can take control of your financial future and achieve the life you desire.

We have discussed the benefits of creating "The Yes Plan" budget, how to set SMART financial goals that align with your values and priorities, and strategies for adjustments, increasing your income, and staying motivated and on track.

By developing your "Yes Plan" for your finances, you have learned to gain confidence in your ability by taking control of your finances and making empowered decisions.

By following your "The Yes Plan," you have learned to create a brighter financial future for yourself, your business, and your loved ones and work towards achieving your financial goals.

Remember, budgeting is not about restriction but about empowering yourself to make informed decisions about your money based on your values, priorities, and future goals.

It's about balancing spending on things that bring you joy and saving for your future.

By practicing discipline and staying committed to your budget, you have learned about a new approach called "The Yes Plan" in this book on budgeting.

This method focuses on shifting your mindset towards a positive and proactive approach to managing your finances.

Instead of feeling restricted by a budget, "The Yes Plan" encourages you to say "yes" to your financial goals and dreams by making intentional and informed choices with your money.

Start making positive changes **today**!

The Yes Plan

About the Author

DeLisa Lovett is an author, financial coach, home-buying educator, and business owner of Lovett Investments, LLC.

The Yes Plan - Empowered through Budgeting assists with managing your finances with an emphasis on saying YES to your future. It teaches you strategies on how and when to say Yes to your future purchase decisions based on your life goals. Create the future you want based on your values, priorities, and goals by adjusting your financial decisions based on your "The Yes Plan" budget.

For future reading and to contact her, please visit her on Facebook, Linked In, Instagram, YouTube, Amazon.com, and DeLisaLovett.com.

www.ingramcontent.com/pod-product-compliance
Lightning Source LLC
Chambersburg PA
CBHW030055230526
45471CB00003B/1114